BABYSITTING

FRANCES S. DAYEE

Babysitting

DRAWINGS BY ANNE CANEVARI GREEN

FRANKLIN WATTS
NEW YORK LONDON TORONTO SYDNEY 1990
A VENTURE BOOK

Library of Congress Cataloging-in-Publication Data

Dayee, Frances S.
Babysitting / Frances S. Dayee ; drawings by Anne Canevari Green.
p. cm. — (A Venture book)
Summary: A guide to earning money as a babysitter, with advice on getting customers, safety, and handling emergencies.
ISBN 0-531-10908-9
1. Babysitting—Vocational guidance—United States—Juvenile literature. [1. Babysitting.] I. Green, Anne Canevari, ill.
II. Title.
HQ769.5.D39 1990
649′.1′0248—dc20   89-24773 CIP AC

CONTENTS

BABYSITTING

You are babysitting for three-year-old Dan and four-month-old Heather. While Heather sleeps, you and Dan make him a peanut butter and jelly sandwich for his lunch. He climbs up on a chair to sit at the kitchen table and eat. Then Heather starts to cry. It's time to feed and change her.

You decide to organize everything before you get her. You fix a bottle and put it in the warmer. You mix cereal in a bowl and set it in a dish of warm water. You gather up clean clothes and a diaper, stack them on the bathroom counter, and lay out the diapering pad. Then the telephone rings on your way to get Heather.

The caller wants to talk to Dan's mother. You let the person know that Mrs. Delbert is busy and can't come to the phone right now, but if the person will leave her name and number Mrs. Delbert will get back to her as soon as she can. You write the information on the phone message board, hang up the phone, and turn around just in time to see Dan holding Heather upside down. "Baby crying," he says.

What do you do?

1. Race over and grab Heather?
2. Sit down?
3. Yell, "How did you get that baby?"
4. Talk quietly to Dan?
5. Panic?

In the beginning, Anthony wouldn't have had the slightest idea what to do. Maybe even now, as a savvy sitter, he wouldn't know exactly what to do. But his advice would be, "Keep a cool head," because certainly number five doesn't work. How does Anthony know?

"Once when I was changing a baby's diaper, he started screaming. I thought I had pinned him and he was bleeding to death. I was going to call the neighbors, the paramedics, my mom, the doctor, the world.

"I hadn't pinned him. I probably pinched him. But I scared myself so bad that I scared him and his brother and they were both crying. I finally had to call my mom to find out what to do to get the kids to stop crying."

Since Anthony realizes his fear scared the children, he'd be able to figure out that numbers one and three are not good choices. If you race up to Dan and try to grab Heather, the toddler may anticipate that and drop the baby. If you yell and startle him, the same thing could happen.

Does it surprise you to find out that the correct answers are two and four? Sit down, preferably on the floor. Chances are Dan will automatically bring the baby to you. If he doesn't, speak softly to him about how lucky Heather is to have a big brother like him. Then ask him to bring you the baby.

Once Heather is secure in your arms, tell Dan how much you appreciated his concern for his sister. Tell him you know he wanted to help. Ask him if he would please come get you next time, however, rather than get Heather by himself. Don't be afraid to admit that you probably took a very long time getting to his sister. Even a short time is long to young children.

ENTER BABYSITTER

Every job has a beginning. There is no experience without a beginning. Susan remembers when she was young and applied for a job. The woman said, "Do you have any experience?"

"No," said Susan.

"Sorry," said the woman.

"I've applied at seven places," Susan said. "The answer's always the same. How am I supposed to get experience if no one will let me work?"

The woman shook her head.

But later in the week, Susan got a call from personnel. They liked the fact that she didn't give up. They had to admit that everyone has to start somewhere; they wanted to give her that chance.

No one can predict what his or her beginning is going to be like, but this is how LeVelle began.

LeVelle's eyes light up to match her smile. "My babysitting career started the summer I was ten. I was hired as a mother's helper for an eighteen-month-old child."

The mother, an author, wanted someone to entertain her daughter while she wrote.

"Before I ever watched Yolanda, I went with her several times to the gym with her mother. Her mother thought it would be a good way for me to get to know her."

LeVelle babysat for Yolanda for a long time. "Later, when Yolanda was older, we read books, lots and lots and lots of books. When we weren't reading books, we were playing with her puppet theater or pretending. We played babysitter a lot and she was the babysitter. Then I'd act just like her and she'd say, 'Girls are supposed to be nice,' and I'd say, 'Is that right? I didn't know that.' "

LeVelle, now a senior in high school, has an afternoon job in a dentist's office. Yet she still babysits in the evenings because, "They love me. All the children I babysit for love me. And I love them."

BOYS SIT TOO

"When I first started babysitting," William says, "I just went to the house, put the baby to sleep, and did my homework or amused myself in some way. As I got more jobs, I began to realize it was more fun to play with the baby. Also, the parents like it better. And you get recalls if the child likes you."

William hit the nail on the head when he said the parents like it better. One parent remarked, "The reason I hire a sitter is to watch my children. I'm looking for someone who is interested in them. I don't want someone who is just interested in making money and hanging out."

It doesn't matter if you're a boy or girl. The most important thing to realize is that babysitting is a job. The more effort you put into it, the more rewards you get out of it.

THE FIRST SITTER

It's amazing how many beginnings there are in the world. The first significant one for you was the day you were born. It was also a beginning for your parents. At that moment their focus expanded to include you. To many parents, their child is more important than life itself. If you understand this, you might begin to understand why parents as employers are such strange creatures.

The other thing it might be helpful to realize about parents is that they don't know everything. They are learning every day the same as everyone else. That may seem unbelievable to you, but it's true. One parent shared this insight.

"At the point where I started hiring babysitters, I really wasn't sure what I wanted in a sitter. That's why I wanted to visit Kristen and Joy in their home before I hired them.

"Family values, being careful, taking your job seriously, those things are very important. I felt the interactive element would be good because they came from a large family. They were children who were used to being around other children. I liked that.

"There's so much of it that's gut reaction that it's hard to analyze."

SITTERS' PARENTS

Parents focus much of their energy on teaching their children to be independent. At the same time, since they don't want to see you grow up *too* soon, they focus a lot of energy on keeping you from becoming too independent too quickly. There are a lot of books written on how parents treat their children like children forever. You may never escape that because parents are worrywarts. They know that everyone makes mistakes in life, but they want to save *their* children from this fate.

Parents keep wondering if they gave you all the necessary skills. You'd be surprised at how proud your parents become as they watch you jump the hurdles of beginnings and hear of your successes. They also face those beginnings, but in a different way. This is what one sitter's parent had to say.

"When Renato first started babysitting, I worried. After all, he's just a kid, and look at all the things that can happen. When the compliments from his customers on having such a wonderful, responsible, conscientious son started pouring in, I stopped worrying. It made me look at my son in a new way."

Your parents will look at you in a new way, also. But they are still your parents, so if you need them for support, let them know. This is going to be a hard time in their lives. They are learning to let go. It's another one of those new beginnings.

Does it surprise you that your beginning will be the beginning for so many others? Even the child you sit for will have a beginning. And you have the power to make it a good one.

CHAPTER

A PROFESSION

You are hired to care for a six-month-old child while his parents go out to dinner. The mother insists you come over two hours early. This is her first child, and this is their first separation since the baby's birth. She walks and talks you through the child's normal evening routine. Routine, she tells you, is very important to a child's development. Doing things the same way and in a particular order, all the time, gives children a sense of security. The mother even demonstrates her method of diapering, feeding, burping, and holding her baby. You come to the conclusion that you cannot live up to this woman's expectations.

What do you do?

1. Refuse to sit?
2. Explain that you will be happy to sit but you can't promise to do everything just as she does?
3. Give her the impression you will do what she wants and then do everything your way?

4. Try to follow the routine but don't worry if things get out of order as long as the baby is happy?
5. Sit once and see how it goes?

There are four acceptable answers. The only one that is not acceptable is number three. The reason? As an employee, it is your responsibility to follow directions to the best of your ability. But if what the parents expect is unreasonable, the best alternative is to refuse to sit. It's preferable to do this rather than be deceitful and pretend to do things the parents' way.

Tera was three months old when Phyllis, a single parent, had to go back to work. "I had the sitter come over a couple of days ahead of time," Phyllis says. "I spent hours showing her exactly how I took care of Tera. I thought nobody could take care of her the way I could."

Looking back, Phyllis says she can see how foolish she was. "I was lucky my sitter didn't quit. After a while I settled down. Tera was happy. That made me happy."

Did the sitter do everything her way? "No, but she tried."

Babysitting is a job you can be proud of. Good babysitters are trustworthy; they know how to follow directions; they have experience in getting along with others, adults and children; they are reliable.

There is no shortage of babysitting jobs for boys or girls. But if the only reason you want to babysit is to make money, think again. This compound word, *babysitting,* is misleading. Taking care of babies is the exception rather than the rule. And sitting is the last position parents or their offspring want to see the childcare giver in.

"It's important to me that the babysitter play with my daughter and interact with her," says Ms. Doyle. "One of the good things about Dana's opportunity to be with a young sitter is that a young person is more likely to play with Dana rather than watch her play. I play with Dana as much as I can, but children can play with children in a way that adults can't just by the nature and proximity of their ages.

"I'm interested in active interaction rather than passive, and it's important to me that there's some initiative in the interactive play experience."

One of the most important qualities a babysitter must have is the ability to like children. Do you have sisters and brothers? Do you get along with them? Do you know how to make them feel better if they are upset? Did you take care of them before they were old enough to tease you into a bad mood? Did you enjoy playing with them when they were little?

If you screwed up your nose at the words *sisters* and *brothers*, that doesn't mean you don't like children. Sisters and brothers live with you and know how to upset you. One of the hardest babysitting jobs you'll ever have is sitting with siblings.

Having sisters and brothers does not automatically qualify you as a babysitter, of course. There are just as many sitters who are only children, or the youngest child, and they make excellent babysitters. But one reason they are good babysitters is that they like children.

KNOW YOURSELF

How do you find out if you like children? The best way to find out is to be around them. Park and

recreation centers can always use volunteers to help with small children. Call day care facilities and ask if they can use a volunteer.

More and more schools have extended day care programs for students. Inquire at your neighborhood school. Check the churches or synagogues in your neighborhood to see if they furnish babysitting for parents who don't want the distraction of children during services.

Volunteer babysitting has several advantages. You can find out whether or not you like working with youngsters. If you find out you love working with children, you'll know babysitting's worth pursuing. This can also open up the possibility for examining professional roles in adulthood, like teaching, for instance.

(On the other hand, if you find you don't really like being around children, babysitting is not for you.)

It's helpful to know which age group a sitter is more comfortable with. An advantage of being a volunteer is that you can work with children of several different age groups.

Eighteen-year-old Joseph confessed, "I like little kids. Not big kids. I babysat for some kids who were perfect angels while their parents were home. When the parents left, they were hyper little brats. I worried the whole time that they were going to get hurt, but I couldn't control them. I didn't go back." Joseph was careful, after that, to find out the ages of the children before he accepted a job.

The only way to establish which age group is your favorite is by interacting with them. Bette thought she'd prefer babies. After taking care of a few infants, she realized that she became impatient when she didn't know why the infant was crying. It also bothered her that people told her that she'd recognize the different cries a baby makes. When she couldn't tell the cries apart, she felt inadequate. Now she sits for, "Kids who talk. They can tell me what they like and don't like, what they want and don't want. Baby detective work was not for me."

William discovered, over time, that his favorite age for a child is one and a half to two. "They like you just the way you are," he says. "No peer pressure. It's great!"

In addition to learning about children, volunteering shows interest. People don't stick around if they don't like the work. If you're a good volunteer babysitter, it will be noticed. Don't be shy about requesting a letter of recommendation. When you're applying for a paid position, a letter like this makes a good impression.

Another way to make a good impression and to develop competence is to take a babysitting class. Few courses give potential sitters an opportunity to work with children, but they do offer valuable background information, especially if you are inexperienced.

If you're interested in taking a babysitting class, call your local Red Cross. They usually know where courses are being offered. Then talk to the organization offering the course and find out what is being covered.

For instance, if you call Campfire Girls and Boys, you'll learn that as well as a beginner babysitting class, Campfire offers a Special Sitters class.

Special Sitters focuses on the needs of persons who are developmentally slow and disabled. Youngsters who wish to take this class must be experienced babysitters and/or have an interest in working with disabled youngsters. The course covers advanced communication skills, including some sign language, and wheelchair handling. Usually the class series ends with a get-together for graduates and their potential clients, who may or may not have already met during the course. The teens who complete the course with a continued desire to work with the disabled are referred to parents of special children.

The criteria for taking a Campfire sitter class, the fee schedule, the timetable, and the method used to teach a babysitting series varies from council to council. So make that call.

CHAPTER

⚑ **three** ⚑

FINDING
EMPLOYMENT

Patricia took a babysitting class at her local children's hospital. The class was for two hours on three consecutive Saturdays. In the first class, she learned about caring for babies. When she was tested on diapering a life-sized doll, safety was an important issue. The second session covered basic first aid, nutrition, and tips on how to play with children of differing ages. The third session covered general and safety-related problems and solutions. Upon completion of the class, Patricia received a certificate of completion. But a certificate is not a job.

How can Patricia find a job?

1. Put an ad in the school newsletter?
2. Go door to door in her neighborhood?
3. Ask her babysitting friends to recommend her?
4. Post an ad on the grocer's bulletin board?
5. Have her relatives spread the word?

Deciding you want to be a babysitter doesn't make it so. You need clients. All the above suggestions are good ones if Patricia lives in a small town where everyone knows everyone else. But if she lives anywhere else, it's not wise to post an ad in a grocery store. The reason is safety.

Safety is an issue that you cannot afford to overlook. Discuss with your parents or other responsible adults safe, effective ways of advertising your services. Going door to door in your neighborhood to the homes of people you know have children may be acceptable to your parents because they prefer you having jobs close to home. Advertising in your school newsletter is all right because the only people who see it are in school. Another way to find a babysitting job is to talk to your babysitting friends. Ask them to recommend you the next time they get a job offer they can't accept. A good babysitter is always in demand.

Even when people seem safe and familiar, it doesn't hurt to have potential employers screened by someone. The most logical screeners are people who love you, who are concerned about your welfare, and who are more experienced in life.

When Jill took her babysitting class at a local recreation center, she was placed on a babysitter referral list. "Before my parents would allow my name on the list, they made me promise to let them talk to referred clients before I did," she said. "I didn't mind. After all, there was no way we could know everyone who came to the rec center. It made me feel safer."

Marie felt safe when she answered an ad in her church bulletin. The job was for an after-school day care person in the parish school. Marie wrote a resume that listed jobs she had held and character references. She wore her best clothes and a smile for the interview. Before she left the interview she was told that even if she didn't get the job, they wanted her to know she had done an excellent job of preparing for the interview.

Andy doesn't have to worry about interviews. He gets his jobs just by being the brother of a long line of highly qualified sister and brother babysitters. But keeping those jobs depends on him.

Another way that Andy is lucky is that his employers are already known to his parents. Parents are less comfortable when your employers are strangers. And, yes, you do have to deal with your parents.

Mr. Kirby wants to meet the family whom his daughter will babysit for in advance. "I can tell a lot about a family when I walk into the house. There is a warmth or coldness about the place, and I'm not talking about heat." If, for some reason, Mr. Kirby can't meet the family, he wants to know how they found out his daughter babysits. That information tells him a lot about the family, also. "I don't always interfere in Bev's business, but I feel I have a right to put my two cents in. After all, it's her safety I'm concerned about."

In case you think it's childish or inappropriate to let your parents or another adult screen prospective employers, it may interest you to know that even professional nanny services check out the people interested in hiring their child care givers. The screener asks questions that will help him or her discover potential problems. For example, a nanny may not want to be employed by a family with smokers or the other way around. Or the parents may be day sleepers and the nanny would have to keep the children quiet all the time. Some nannies wouldn't be able to handle that. Even after the employee is placed with a family, if a problem arises between the nanny and an employer that they can't solve between themselves, the service will act as a mediator.

BEFORE YOU GET
THE JOB

Even before the interview, there are a few things you need to know. First, what do your parents expect of you? One parent who supplies babysitters put it this way.

> My youngsters are to check with their father or me before they accept a job. We want to be sure there is nothing on the calendar that interferes with responsibility or commitment to family. They have to write down the person's name and phone number so I can reach them. During the week they're supposed to be home by 9:00 P.M. If they are scheduled to babysit until 9:00 and the couple gets home at 9:30, that may be okay. But, if that couple keeps them late on a regular basis, they may have to talk to the people and tell them they can't babysit for them anymore. On weekends my kids may babysit until 12:30 A.M., or if it's someone we know, we'll talk things over and certain arrangements can be made.

Many an argument has erupted between parents and babysitting youngsters because of a misunderstanding in expectations. Talk things over in advance with your parent. This doesn't guarantee smooth sailing all the time—unexpected, unexplored situations may still come up. But, on the whole, it pays to try to work your jobs around and within parental schedules, guidelines, and expectations.

Find out where your parents want the name, address, and phone number of your employer kept for easy reference. One parent said, "We have a book. If it's not in the book, they don't go."

Another parent pointed to a large wall calendar. "Everything that's scheduled goes on this calendar. Whether they schedule it or I schedule it, everything is written down so I know exactly where I stand and where they are. If it's a long day, say in the summer, then the person who is sitting calls to say, 'If I'm gone, I'm at the park,' or whatever, so I have an idea what's going on. No matter where they are, I know."

One young girl found it a definite advantage to know where her mother was when the girl was babysitting. "Mom lets me know where to reach her if she's not going to be home. One time I called her at my grandmother's because the toilet was plugged up and I couldn't find the plunger. Getting a hold of her saved the day."

If you're from a family of babysitters, the advantage is that your parents are already trained to some extent. The disadvantage is they might need your services at home. One mother states, "I realize that's how Helen makes her money, but her primary concern is to be here when I need her. She figures I'm the one who got myself into this situation (all those little ones running around). Why should she have any responsibility in it? I see her point and I try not to take advantage of her, but home, family, is always first."

If things aren't perfect, be willing to compromise. Sometimes the excitement of being an independent business person and the building up of a cash flow override good sense. Even if you

don't have chores you are responsible for around the house, time for homework, social life, and sleep needs to be scheduled into the babysitting agenda.

A person who is not well rested or is stressed by lack of time for friends and homework does not do well with children. In fact, stress is probably the main reason *parents* give for wanting to take a break from their children. They need the time away to refocus and refresh themselves.

CHAPTER

HOW MUCH
TO CHARGE

"I really like a babysitter to tell me what he or she expects to be paid, and not say, 'I don't know' or 'I don't care.' "

Most babysitters have an idea what they would like to be paid, but they are uncomfortable talking about money. In 1964 the going rate for a babysitter was fifty cents an hour. Today that sounds like pioneer-day prices. In 1980 one mother's helper received a dollar an hour. When she graduated to babysitting status her pay was raised to $1.50 an hour.

Many people will try to get the least-expensive sitter they can because admission to any event and dining out, plus a babysitting fee, can break the bank for young parents.

Mr. and Mrs. Lowell have two sets of twins sixteen months apart. "I need someone who is willing to take a reasonable rate of pay," says Mrs. Lowell, "or we can't go out. I think sitters should be willing to understand the financial needs of the family they are sitting for."

Every babysitter has encountered this kind of

ANNE CANEVARI GREEN

family. It is hard to argue with their logic when the babysitter is a luxury.

Krista admits she is willing to take on a job for less money, "When I don't do anything but play with the kids. But it's hard to find kids that good, and I charge more for kids who are difficult to handle."

Roberto, an experienced babysitter, charges a base price per hour for one child, doubles it for two children, then adds fifty cents for each additional child. But he remembers the time when he took what he could get. "With experience, my employers raised my pay. Then I charged the higher fee to new customers."

A good babysitter is definitely a treasure, so don't sell yourself short and undercharge. Expect fair payment while charging a fair price.

Babysitting prices may differ as much as fifty cents to a dollar per hour from one part of town to another. Do some detective work. What do your friends charge? What does your sister or brother charge? What do babysitting instructors suggest as the going rate? Talk to your teachers. Ask them what they think. Many of them have children, so they would know firsthand. Call some people who have children. Ask them what they pay and what they think is fair. Experience counts. Classes in first aid and babysitting count.

Mrs. Myron says, "I think babysitters should be paid well and I think they should feel good about that. I'll pay anything they are charging if they're good."

Mrs. Myron admits the key word is *good*. Youngsters who have had babysitters and parents who pay for the services defined *good* as someone who plays or does things with the children and likes children.

Once you decide what you want to charge, make it a point to bring up your fee the first time you are called. "I charge two dollars an hour until midnight. Then my fee goes up to three dollars an hour."

If the rate seems high to a potential employer, he'll say so. In that case, you have three choices.

The first is to refuse the job in hopes of getting another offer with someone who is willing to pay your rate.

The second choice is to try for a compromise. If you're offered $1.50 an hour, request $1.75.

The third choice is to accept $1.50. Taking less from one customer doesn't mean you can't charge another customer what you believe you deserve.

In fact, there are occasions when taking less is the smart thing to do. Lowering your price to meet others' needs may create more business. Happy customers brag about their babysitters. Also, when customers feel they are getting a bargain, they'll call you more often.

There's an old saying, "A bird in the hand is worth two in the bush." It means sometimes you're better off taking what you can get rather than waiting around for what you might get.

As a business person, you have the right to weigh the advantages and disadvantages of taking less money. Sometimes a lower-paying customer makes up for it by leaving a special snack for you in the kitchen or remembering you on birthdays and holidays.

KEEPING A FILE

It will help you to keep a record of your customers. This is easy to set up. Buy a small file box, a package of 3 × 5 cards, and a set of alphabet index

cards. A writer friend keeps a record of reference sources and people he interviews. He sets relevant information up this way:

Name

Phone number

Address

City, State, Zip Code

Under the phone number, you might want to put the date you were first contacted and how much you're charging that customer. Maybe you'll want to skip a couple of lines and list the names and ages of the children. At the bottom of the card you might note how the person found out you baby-sit: recommended by _____ ; answered ad; friend of family; door-to-door canvas.

Record relevant information somewhere on the card. Do the customers need you every Wednesday and Friday? Does this employer expect the children to be given a bath before they go to bed? Do the people come home when they say they will or are they always late? Do their checks bounce? Is there too much expected of you? Are there too many children for one sitter? Are the children great, good, okay, difficult? Are the parents easy or hard to work for? If you can't sit for them, would you recommend a friend?

You might even want to rate customers on a scale of one to ten—one being low and ten being high—the first few times you babysit. If their rate is always under a six, it might be wise to drop them. Adults who take advantage of you on a regular basis or treat you badly don't deserve your services.

A "THINK ABOUT IT" STORY

Carmen, a sophomore in high school, received the name and phone number of a potential summer employer from her school counselor.

When she called to set up the interview, she learned that she'd be watching four-year-old Kevin and two-year-old Dotty weekday mornings for about five hours while the husband worked and the wife went to school. The father said he'd conduct the interview and that it would take a couple of hours. He wanted to see how Carmen and the children got along. He also requested that Carmen bring references. Carmen agreed that interacting with the children was a good idea and assured him that references weren't a problem.

When Carmen arrived for the interview, the children were playing. "The father was all business," Carmen remembers. "Not at all what I was used to. But then, I'd never interviewed with a father before. Just mothers. I handed him my references. While he looked at them, I talked to the kids. I was really nervous.

"He asked me if I had any special talents or

knew any foreign languages. I admitted that I did calligraphy, knew a bit of sign language, and was taking Spanish. He said it would be nice if I passed this knowledge on to the children. I thought the kids would enjoy doing sign language, and that made me excited.

"The father let me know that I'd be expected to get the kids up in the morning, and wash, dress, and feed them. He said that they were to rest about halfway through the morning, and that *if* I had time, it would be nice if I vacuumed the floors and folded the clothes in the dryer. But I was *never*, under *any* circumstances, to leave *either* of the children *alone*. If one child was sleeping upstairs, I was to stay there and entertain the other child until both were awake. He said he was *very* concerned that his children were *well* taken care of.

"We discussed salary. I would be paid once a week *if* I was hired. He said punctuality was a *must*, and that I was to be there at 6:30 A.M. He said that he and his wife didn't leave until around 7:30, but I needed to be there in case one of the kids woke up.

"During the interview, I always felt a little off balance, but I thought it was just because the father was so serious.

"Before I left, I read Kevin and Dotty a book. They were like normal kids, listening sometimes and jumping off the sofa to play with a toy at other times. I showed them some finger games and got a kick out of watching them try to do them. They weren't at all shy with me.

"As I left, their father handed me a sheet of paper. When I got home, I realized it was a schedule, practically by the minute, for the kids, and a list of suggested learning activities and experiences."

The job wouldn't start for three weeks, so Carmen lost herself in studying for finals. But when Carmen hadn't heard from the potential employer by the last day of school, she felt unsettled. She definitely wanted a summer job, but she felt she couldn't apply for another one while the first job was on hold. Yet every time Carmen looked at the phone, she saw the man's critical eyes staring at her. Carmen thought he'd think she was rushing him. Finally, she asked her mother to make the call.

Mrs. Tavernini told the man that Carmen needed to know if she had the job or if she should apply elsewhere. The father promised to make a decision before the day ended.

That evening he called to tell Carmen she got the job. He said he'd see her Monday. He emphasized that she be on time.

On Monday, the father greeted Carmen at the door.

"He started out by showing me where the dryer was, how to fold the clothes, and where to put them. Then he showed me the kitchen. All the time it was show and tell, show and tell. What the kids could eat, what time they had to eat, and what to do if they didn't eat. We're pretty relaxed at home, even though Mom doesn't like to see food wasted. But this guy made it a federal offense if you didn't finish what was put in front of you. I was glad *I* didn't eat there.

"Even after the kids got up, he stood over me and told me what to do and not do. He was in total command, and it sounded like he wanted me to be in total command, too. A lot of stuff he said was on the paper he'd given me to study at home. But he continued to add stuff that wasn't on the paper. I stopped trying to remember everything he was saying a few minutes after the kids were up. I couldn't keep up with him and the kids, too."

Carmen was still excited about having a summer job with afternoon freedom. She figured that once the Mr. was gone and she was in charge instead of taking orders, everything would be fine.

The first week, everything was fine. Carmen arrived early each day, filled with enthusiasm. She set the table for the children's breakfast and decided what they were having. She found she had time on her hands, so Carmen folded clothes just because they were there, *and* he'd said, "*If* you have the time." But Carmen was uncomfortable folding other people's clothes. It was too personal.

She got the vacuuming done by making it a game with the youngsters. But the days were very full, and she was exhausted when she got home. She figured things would get better when she'd worked out a routine. Things are always hard when you start a new job.

One day Carmen couldn't get the vacuuming done because she couldn't do it when the children were asleep and there just wasn't any other time. She apologized and explained. The youngsters' father said it was perfectly understandable.

The next week she brought a summer reading book to keep her occupied until the children got up, since it bothered her more and more to handle other people's personal clothing. She decided *if* she had time, she'd fold the clothing, but only children's clothes and diapers.

Beginning the new week, Carmen felt comfortable with the children. She was working her way into a schedule and learning more about the youngsters' likes and dislikes. She also saw that the children were acting more like themselves with her. At first, they had done or eaten what she'd suggested. Now they were making choices.

One time when Carmen changed Dotty, she put the baby's messy diaper by the toilet. While Carmen was doing this, Kevin ran off. Carmen heard the father's forceful voice in her mind, reminding her not to leave a child alone for an instant. She threw a towel around Dotty and chased after Kevin. Kevin thought it was a great game.

When the father came home, Carmen remembered, "He yelled at me. He was angry that I'd left the diaper [by the toilet]. I apologized, but he wouldn't listen or give me time to explain. He was angry that I read in the morning instead of folding clothes. He was angry because the vacuuming wasn't always done. He demanded to know what I was doing all day. He accused me of reading instead of paying attention to the kids.

"I started crying, told him he was wrong, and left. I went home and told Mom. She thought maybe I was overreacting. She wanted me to calm down, call my employer, and request time to talk things over rationally.

"When I agreed, Mom drove me over and sat in the car while I talked inside the house. He rationalized. Before I left, I was convinced I was wrong and he was right and everything would be okay if I just did what I was supposed to do.

"The next day Kevin told me I wasn't his mommy or daddy and I couldn't tell him what to do, and if I didn't let him do what he wanted, he was going to have his daddy fire me.

"I told him to be my guest. I didn't think he could seriously do it, but it bothered me that he felt he could treat me that way."

As one day melted into the other, Carmen was

more and more on edge. Kevin was uncoopera-
tive. Carmen went to the child's father for advice.
In a demanding tone, in front of the children, he
said, "You must always be in control!"

Carmen started to put Kevin on a chair for
"time-outs." Her mother had told her that a child
can only sit for one minute for each year of age,
so Carmen limited Kevin to four minutes. But he
misbehaved so often that he was in the chair more
than he was out, and he would only sit unsupervised for thirty seconds. Dotty received less attention because of Kevin, and Carmen found it more
and more difficult to keep up with picking up after
the youngsters, much less doing the extra chores.

The father criticized Carmen more and more
for the cluttered front room. When she picked up
toys before leaving, he'd complain because she
didn't have the children help her.

One day Carmen cried all the way home. She
was nearly hysterical when she complained to her
mom that the man never complimented her, he
only criticized. She was angry that he expected
her to do things that he'd previously told her to
do only, "*If* you have time." And she resented the
fact that the children's father criticized her in front
of the children. She felt that Kevin's misbehavior
was directly related to the way his father treated
her.

After Carmen calmed down, she decided to talk
to the father again. She screwed up her courage
and told him one morning, as he left for work,
that she wanted a conference. Then she called and
asked her mother to be waiting in the car if she
needed her.

When the children's father returned, Carmen
said, "I don't want to be responsible for folding
clothes, vacuuming, or any other household chores

because it wasn't in the job description. You said *if* I had time. I don't."

Carmen felt that the man was trying to intimidate her. He glared at her and said, "You are here at 6:30. The children don't get up until after 7:30. Look at my position. If I pay someone, I have a right to expect them to earn their salary. If you have a job, you have to learn responsibility. If you want to keep your job, you perform your duties. If you don't have anything to do, you find something to do. I'm just, after all, supplying you with busy work."

"I wasn't hired to do household chores," Carmen insisted. "I don't want busy work. I just want to take care of the children. I can come later so you don't have to pay me for that hour."

There was a long pause.

"All right. Come a half hour later."

Carmen was elated. She hadn't let the man intimidate her, and she'd easily fill that half hour with child-related duties. Now, she assumed "busy work" was a thing of the past.

The next day she let herself into the house, picked out the youngster's clothes, and set the table. The father found her in the kitchen and told her Kevin was having his tonsils removed and since she only had one child, he wanted her to vacuum.

"I thought I made it clear that I didn't want 'busy work,' " Carmen answered. "I am busy enough taking care of the children and keeping up with your written schedule."

He repeated that she only had one child and Dotty wasn't that difficult to watch.

"That's not the point," Carmen insisted, "I thought we established that I was only hired to babysit. If you want me to do housework, then I expect to be paid extra."

His face turned scarlet. "Consider this your last day," he spat and slammed out the door.

Carmen felt like she'd just dumped a thousand-pound rock. "I was proud that I'd finally stood up for myself and what I believed."

Within a half an hour the father was back and had paid her off. Carmen didn't know it could feel so good to be fired.

There are no good guys or bad guys in this story. But, since the father wanted someone to command, teach, clean house, keep to a strict schedule, and follow his rules, an adult with a military background might have been a better choice than a high school student.

Carmen was serious about her role as caretaker, but her more relaxed attitude reflected the environment she grew up in.

It took all her courage to stand up to a person who went from "*if* you have time" to expecting the job to be done. Even a great deal of babysitting didn't prepare her for this situation.

As a result of this experience, Carmen makes it clear to potential employers that she limits her job to babysitting.

"If the parents want a tutor, they can hire one. If they want a housekeeper, they can get one of them, too. I'm just taking care of the kids.

"That doesn't mean I won't teach them something. My mom says just by being there I teach them. Kids are listening all the time. And, if I'm only babysitting, it doesn't mean there won't be any cleaning. If the kids eat at the table and leave a mess, I'll wipe the table, maybe even end up sweeping the kitchen floor. If we make cookies, we have to clean up after ourselves."

A sitter's first responsibility is to the child. If part of the job is picking up toys after a child is done playing with them or seeing that the child does it, that's acceptable. If it's changing a wet sheet for a dry one before a child takes a nap or helping potty-train little Jenny, that's acceptable. If it's washing the dishes that were dirtied while giving the child a meal, that's acceptable.

But, being expected to strip all the beds and remake them is not acceptable. Duties that include doing the family laundry and/or washing a week's worth of dishes are not acceptable. Even if you are being paid extra, any job that distracts your attention from the child may not be acceptable. Watching a child is a full-time job, even for adults.

Though you have the right to be respected as a professional, extra responsibility is not necessarily the way to show respect. It's easy to confuse responsibility with dependability. Dependability means you are trustworthy. You can be trusted to do a good job. Responsibility often just means more work. When more work makes you feel as though you've been taken advantage of, it's easy to become resentful. Savvy sitters have learned that when they're resentful, they're unhappy and they don't do a good job.

CHAPTER

 ⚜ **SIX** ⚜

INTERVIEWING

Although the dictionary defines an interview as a face-to-face meeting arranged for formal discussion, the truth is, most babysitting interviews take place on the phone and seem to be more of an interrogation than a discussion. Keep the dictionary definition in mind and feel free to politely ask for as much information as you feel you need.

Interviews are unsettling. One way to become more confident is to interview yourself in the mirror or have a friend play the role of a prospective employer. Answering questions aloud helps you decide if the response is what you want to say, the way you want to say it. Taking time to practice smooths out the rough spots and makes you more comfortable. When you're comfortable, you are yourself. Being yourself is the best person you can be.

Another thing you can do for yourself is to write out questions and/or personal guidelines you wish to discuss with the employer.

How do you feel about babysitting for children who are ill? How do your parents feel? If you talk

ANNE CANEVARI GREEN

to your parents and they decide they do not want you to sit for children who have something contagious, it's fair to establish an "I don't babysit children who are contagious" guideline. Neither schools nor day care facilities want sick children to attend because sickness spreads. Your health and the health of your family are important.

Of course, that goes both ways. If you are ill, don't spread your germs to another family. Call as soon as you can to cancel. If you have a list of babysitting friends, share that with your employer.

You might want to consider instituting a cancellation fee. One young lady only charged a fee if she had turned down another job, but professionals from hairdressers to doctors and dentists charge a fee for broken appointments without twenty-four hours' notice.

While you're writing out questions or guidelines for the customer, think of questions they may ask you and prepare yourself with written answers. A parent may want to know what experience you've had, the names of some people who would give you a good recommendation (are these at your fingertips?), and what you charge.

If you haven't had any experience, be honest. Tell the caller instead why you would make a good babysitter. Suggest the names of people who would be glad to supply a good character reference. A teacher, a neighbor, one of your parent's friends or one of your friend's parents are all good sources. It's always wise to ask in advance if you may use people as a reference. It gives them time to think about all your good qualities.

Before you discuss your fee, ask how many children you will be responsible for, their ages, and what your *exact* duties will be. If customers want you to do more than babysit, decide if it's fair or unreasonable. If it seems like too much work, tell them that when you sit, you limit yourself to sitting, and for sitting you charge $____ an hour. Politely let them know that if they want you to do housework, you will be glad to clean on a day when you aren't sitting and that you charge $____ an hour. If they aren't satisfied with those responses, the interview will be over.

There are always mixed feelings when you don't get a job. But when more is expected of you than you can comfortably deliver, you are better off without that job. Once you start a job, if you find out the duties are more than you can handle, it's difficult to admit and often creates hard feelings.

Adults who are upset when a younger person politely stands up for his or her rights spell trouble. Most adults will respect your ability to speak up and establish limits. They are very aware that everyone is not capable of everything, and quality care for their children is a priority. This type of person may end up hiring you to do the extra jobs another time. The people who respect your job guidelines are the employers you want.

Before you accept a job, find out where the people live and what hours they need you. It's important to know if the job is too far away or in a neighborhood where your parents wouldn't let you babysit anyway. It's always acceptable for you to limit how far away from home you want to babysit. It may not seem like a big deal until you find that transportation time eats into free time or you're losing jobs because you can't get home soon enough. Then time becomes a priority, and close to home saves time.

Also, if you decide you'd like to take a job that is miles from home, clear it with your parents *before* you accept. Even though the babysitting business is your business, parents have a right to make decisions that affect your safety. By making it a policy to clear jobs with them, you can avoid the embarrassment of having to cancel out on someone after you've promised to sit. Don't expect your parents to automatically supply transportation for you. That's a detail that needs to be worked out, not assumed, beforehand.

You have taken a sitting job that's within walking distance of home. It is your responsibility to meet the two children at the bus stop at 3:00 P.M. four days a week and walk them home. You are also expected to make an after-school snack for them since neither parent will be home before six.

Within the first few days, you see that the parents aren't showing up before 6:15 and usually after 6:30. You agreed to the job based on their getting home by six. You counted on this because you are in the school play, practice is at 7:00, and your mother insists you eat before you go. You tell her you don't have time and she says, "If you don't have time to eat, it appears you must make time. If you can't work it out, you'll have to choose between the play and the job."

How do you handle this situation?

1. You have a tantrum and run to your room?
2. You do nothing?
3. You call your customers and tell them you can't sit?
4. You quit the play?
5. You compromise?

ANNE CANEVARI GREEN

Any self-respecting babysitter knows number one isn't the answer. Andrea says, "When kids I sit for have a temper tantrum, I make sure there's nothing around them they can get hurt on. Then I walk out of the room and wait nearby for them to stop. After they stop, I say, 'If you want something, that's not the way to get it.' "

The do-nothing method (number 2) doesn't work either. If you don't do something, your parents will.

The problem with number three is that quitting could cause you embarrassment. In addition, out of courtesy, it's only fair to give an employer time to find a replacement sitter, so this solution could take at least two weeks.

Yes, you could quit the play (number 4). That will please your mother and solve the time problem. But how will it make you feel? If being in the play means a lot to you, it may be a big sacrifice. Are you going to take your resentment out on others? If you are, then you'll have to rethink this one.

Compromise (number 5) is the best solution.

Maybe just presenting the problem will create a solution. Adults were young once. They know what the school play means or that special dance or the softball game. If they know what the problem is, with enough advance notice, often it can be solved. The trick is to bring it up as soon as you know.

There's an old saying, "A stitch in time saves nine." It means the sooner a problem is uncovered, the easier it is to solve; a problem left unsolved gets out of hand.

Most employers prefer to know all the facts, because it not only avoids problems, but it saves time. So, if this is an evening job, and you don't sit past 9:00 P.M. Monday through Thursday because of school, say so. If you have orthodontist appointments once a month so they may need a replacement babysitter, or you have piano lessons once a week and you may need a ride to the lesson if you sit, run it by them. If you can't sit past midnight on Fridays without special arrangements from your parents, and you don't sit on Sunday because it's family day, if you're a good babysitter you'll still have plenty of jobs. Parents work around a good babysitter's schedule.

It's also a good idea to bring up any fears that may affect your ability to do a good job. Are you afraid of water? If the family has a pool, you may be better off not sitting for them. Are you afraid of heights? If they have a house of many stories with a circular staircase, it could immobilize you.

Are you afraid of any kind of animal? Customers often don't think to mention pets because they are just an everyday thing in the house, like the fact that the front room is blue or the bathroom is tiled. Because of this, you may have to become an investigator.

By the same token, customers who own unusual pets should let you know. Michelle babysat for some children who revealed they had a boa constrictor. "It gave me a creepy feeling to know that thing was in the house. All night I expected it to slither up to me. I was skittery all the time the kids were up, but I tried not to let them know. If they knew I was freaked, they might have let it out.

"After they were in bed, I sat with my feet under me and watched the door to the room the snake was in. I never went back to that house again."

Michelle's sister, Colleen, couldn't wait for the people to call again. When they did, she took the job and asked to hold the reptile. Yet both girls agreed that it wasn't fair that the customers didn't tell them that they had a snake.

If you're allergic to cats, it won't do to take a sitting job where there's a cat. And if you're deathly afraid of dogs, you don't need much advice about that.

If you're just moderately afraid of dogs, you might be able to establish a relationship with the animal, the same way you do with the children, by visiting ahead of time. If you can't, then request that the animal be put away in a room, locked in the basement, or retired to the backyard. If you're still not comfortable, take a page out of Michelle's book—don't sit.

One more thing about dogs. It's important to know as much as you can about the animal. So, ask questions. Grandmother Berkley was visiting some friends with a large family and a *big* dog. The children's mother asked Grandma if she could keep an eye on the sleeping children. The mother didn't want to wake them, but she needed to pick up the schoolchildren. Grandma agreed.

"Everything was fine," Grandma says, "until I went out to get the paper. When I tried to get back in, the dog growled. I tried talking to him. He attacked the door. I closed the door and sat on the front porch until the mother returned."

A dog will sometimes be very friendly when you are invited inside the house by his owners, and even be glad to accept you if the owners leave. But find out if the friendliness is merely on the surface. An animal who is overly protective is nothing to fool around with. You have no defenses against a surprise attack.

CHAPTER

BREAKING
THE ICE

Visiting the children and the household before you actually babysit is a good policy, whether it's the customer's idea or yours. Children are more comfortable with someone they have met before, and you can evaluate your employers, your charges, and your surroundings before you are actually employed.

To make a good impression when visiting, dress in neat, clean clothes that say you are prepared to play. Put a smile on your face and pay attention to the child or children.

Mrs. Nagaishi says, "I look for someone who walks into my house and immediately notices my children. Someone who gets eye contact and talks to them. Tries to get to know them."

This employer's advice is useful for any age child. Babies may not talk, but they love to hear voices, and they see better than many people believe. Infants are partial to bright colors and rhythm. They like singing, even if it's off key, and rocking.

Preschool children also may not talk, but they are always interested in new things and people. Usually there's no in-between personality at this age. The child is either very outgoing or very shy. And, the outgoing child may not be outgoing toward the babysitter. He or she likes parents best. The secret is to not rush things. Let the child come to you.

One way to get a preschooler's attention is by using a hand puppet. It's easier for children to interact with a puppet than a person. If you can tell that the child is very shy, sit on something low so you look smaller and have the puppet introduce himself or herself and you. Then have the puppet say something like, "_____ doesn't bite or scratch or pick his/her nose. Do you?" Very shy children usually at least shake their heads. Let the puppet look around, wave, or talk to you. Be aware of the child's actions so the puppet can respond when necessary.

Once you overcome preschoolers' shyness, listen. Their logic is amazing.

One Saturday after a get-acquainted playtime with three-year-old Wanda, Bernice suggested they read a book. "Then I have to leave," she said.

The tot ran to her, gave her a hug, and said, "Don't go. I want to play more."

"I'm glad you want me to stay and I promise I'll come again. But after we read the book, I have to go home and do my chores."

"What's chores?" Wanda asked.

"My work. I have to do things like wash dishes, clean the table, sweep the floor, fold clothes. . . ."

"Like Cinderella?"

If children are old enough to walk, they are also old enough to show you where their toys and clothes are. When children know something you don't, it makes them feel important. Children want to be recognized. Ask them about their toys and if they have a favorite.

School-age children like tricks and magic. You'll have their attention if you can make a coin appear and disappear, fool them with cards, or surprise them with toothpick tricks and puzzles. If you're going to use this attention getter, there are two things to consider. 1) Keep in mind the age of the child. If it takes too long or is too complicated, you'll lose a young child's attention. 2) Practice, practice, practice. You quickly destroy your credibility if children figure out how the trick's done because it isn't done well. On the other hand, you'll be the hit of the neighborhood if you can fool them and then teach them how to perform magic themselves.

It's hard to put children in a category of interest because each child is so different. Phillip, in the fifth grade, hates to read. Heidi, one of Phillip's classmates, is in the process of teaching herself Chinese.

A game of basketball will put you on Phillip's good side, especially if you can give him some hints on how to beat his dad. On the other hand, Heidi will be proud to show you how Chinese characters often resemble what they represent.

If a sitter can discover the interests of each child on that first visit, he or she will know how to prepare. It's like a game of hide and seek. Some children's interests are easier to discover than others. But once you break the ice and uncover the key to their individuality, you'll know whether to concentrate on being playmate, companion, or friend.

The relationship between you and the children is usually more intimate than the one you develop with the parents. But both relationships are equally important.

Gretta says, "If you get a creepy feeling about the parents, don't babysit. Even though you don't have to be around them much, they can make things pretty uncomfortable. Just say you're busy."

Joey says, "If I don't like the kids' parents, I just tell them my mom and dad said no. Then I tell my parents what's going on so they can back me up."

Sometimes the problem doesn't become obvious until you've been babysitting for a while. It may be something as simple as a personality conflict or as complicated as drug abuse. It's acceptable to turn down a job at any time.

It's also acceptable to tell your friends you won't babysit for a particular family if you feel it's important. The key word is *important*. Before you tell anyone a family is off limits for you, talk it over with a trusted adult to see if they also feel sharing your information is appropriate.

PROFESSIONALS ASK

The younger the child, the more important it is to be able to locate diapers, changing equipment, extra clothes, bed, bedding, and food source. A baby can't say if he or she has a pacifier or a favorite blanket or if the missing blanket is why you're having trouble putting her or him to sleep. He can't tell you if Mom gives him an iced teething ring. She can't show you where her coat and hat are kept.

Spencer has colic. Every night between eight and ten the only thing that comforts him is to be walked. Not rocked, walked. Bonnie sleeps for a half an hour after each feeding and is ready for lots and lots of activities for the next three or so hours, even at night. If you go to either house with a pile of homework expecting to do it while the baby sleeps, it's likely you'll end up doing homework at home.

Why wouldn't the parents tell you about Bonnie's wakefulness or Spencer's colic? Because they are used to it. They live and deal with it every day, and don't see it as out of the ordinary.

So, if colic isn't brought up, don't be afraid to ask. Professionals ask questions. Are there any special problems I should be aware of? If so, what is the best way to handle it? Does the baby have a routine that needs to be followed? If there are dogs or cats in the house, is it okay for them to lick or snuggle with the baby?

Even with babies, there are house rules. Is it okay, during daylight hours, to take the baby for a walk? How far away? If it's acceptable to leave the house, where is the extra key? If you lock yourself out, is there a neighbor who has a key? If the neighbor isn't home, is it okay for you to take the children to your house? If not, what is acceptable?

Some parents, especially new ones, want absolute quiet when the baby is sleeping. Is it okay to have the radio or TV on when the baby is asleep? If not, don't bring your Walkman. The earphones could cover an infant's cry.

The older the child, the more important it is to talk to parents about established house rules. Some children have a built-in urge to test the sitter's house rules' awareness. Your research could mean the difference between calm and conflict.

Is any area of the house off limits? The basement may be out of bounds because of anything from poisons to electric tools that the children cannot use without supervision. The front room may be out of bounds to anyone with food or drink. Parents often declare their bedroom off limits. Television viewing, bedtimes, and snacks can vary from one family to another.

In some families, children are allowed to answer the phone. In others, only the adult or sitter answers the phone. If you're uncomfortable with a child answering the phone, say so.

Some parents will allow the sitter to decide if their child can go to another house to play. Even in this, there are limits. Other families are strict about plans being finalized by the parents. Make sure you have the facts—names, phone numbers, description—and do not, under any circumstances, let a child leave with anyone if the parents don't tell you that the outing was arranged for and approved. It is better to have an angry grandmother than a missing child.

You can't be expected to know another family's house rules unless they are posted, or you have been their regular sitter for a long time. Anything parents feel strongly about, they'll usually mention. For instance, the mother of a preschooler stated, "I feel very strongly about commercial TV. *No! No! No!*"

Some parents of preschool children are more lenient. They allow their children to at least watch children's shows. At the same time, the parents count on their babysitter to use good judgment when it comes to what little ones should watch on TV. What are *your* house rules about TV viewing? Are any shows or TV channels off limits in your family? If the parents you're sitting for don't have strict TV rules, consider the age of the child. Young children are easily frightened. If you are allowed to watch horror shows, watch them at home. Although you may use what you are allowed to do at your home as a guide, remember that rules change from house to house. Never assume. Always ask.

Pete and Carol had made arrangements for their favorite babysitter to watch their sons while they attended a business dinner. The day of the dinner, the sitter became ill. Pete's boss referred to them a high school student who was his

daughter's friend. The girl showed up at the last minute, so Carol showed her where the boys' beds and necessities were, gave her the phone number where they could be reached, and dashed out the door. When the couple returned later that evening, the sitter was sprawled on the floor surrounded by compact disks.

Although Carol hadn't told the girl the CD player was off limits, she felt her privacy had been invaded. "I know the disks are supposed to have a long life," she said, "but only if they are well taken care of. My disks were on the rug, picking up lint, which affects the player. I had them filed on the very top shelf of my bookcase. That girl had to get a stepstool to reach them. I was so upset I had to leave the room and let Pete contend with her. She'll never babysit at my house again."

Not only will she not sit at that house again, but she probably won't ever find out why she isn't asked back. It's mistakes like this that will keep a business from expanding, yet you can't take care of a problem you don't know exists. In this case, the parents did not have time to tell the babysitter not to use the player.

Do your parents have any electronic equipment that no one uses but them? Is there some equipment that you can use *if* you ask permission? If you're familiar with limits, use them as a guide for yourself and your charges. If there's ever a question in your mind whether you or the children are allowed to use certain equipment, the safest decision is *don't* use it. Even if you find it's something that is allowed, parents appreciate it when you clear it with them first.

Another thing to clear with parents is their method of discipline. Joseph said, "I like for the parents to say it in front of the kids. That way they know that I know what to do and have permission to do it and they are more cooperative."

Annette says, "Even if the parents give me permission, I don't hit the kids. I feel hitting them teaches them to hurt others."

If parents don't give any suggestions regarding discipline, most babysitters agree that time spent alone works best for children who misbehave. Depending on the age of the child, sitting on a chair in the same room you are in or going to their room works best. Henry says, "I have them sit on the chair. After about a minute, I talk to them about what they did. Then I give them a hug so they know I'm not going to stay mad at them."

It's just as important, if not more important, to let children know what they do *right*. If you look for the best in them, you'll usually get it.

If you expect to be sitting at night, inquire about children's sleeping habits. Are they afraid of the dark? Do they need a night light? Sometimes a hall light has to be left on until the children are asleep.

Is there a ritual the children follow that makes them more comfortable about going to bed? Some children need to put on their pajamas, have a cookie, brush their teeth, and have two or three books read, in that order. If things are done out of order, they can't sleep.

If a parent tells you that his child is in the habit of going right to sleep and sleeping through the night, but the child won't go to sleep for you, forcing the issue seldom works. Some children are uncomfortable when their parents leave. Ask them if they want to be held or would like for you to lie down with them. If the answer is no, respect their wishes. If they confess to being afraid of ghosts, don't laugh. Ask them if their parents have a se-

YES, JONATHAN, I KNOW THE ROUTINE... HALF GLASS OF MILK IN YOUR BATMAN GLASS, TWO COCONUT COOKIES, YOUR TEDDY BEAR, "THE MIGHTY PUMPKIN" STORY, AND YOUR BLUE BLANKIE...

ANNE CANEVARI GREEN

cret way of getting rid of ghosts. Or tell them about your experience with ghosts, especially if you resolved it.

When Daniel told Julia he was afraid of ghosts, she asked the ghost's name. "It doesn't have one," he said. So Julia told Daniel about her family's pet ghost, Judy. "The best thing about Judy," Julia said, "was that we could blame everything on her. If there was water on the bathroom floor and no one wanted to admit they did it, we blamed Judy."

Daniel decided to name his ghost Grover. Once Grover had a name, he wasn't frightening anymore. He was a friend.

CHAPTER

✣ nine ✣

SAFETY

One of the best things you can do for yourself is to make sure the address (include the cross streets), telephone number, and name of your customer are by the phone or in your pocket. Hand write or type this information so you can read it. This may sound silly, but even adults forget their address and phone number in an emergency. How likely do you think it is that you'll remember the address where you're sitting?

Other information you need to have handy is where to reach the children's parents, whom to call if you can't reach the parents, and the phone numbers for the poison center, the police, the fire department, and the children's doctor. If you are too nervous to dial a phone number, dial 0 for an operator, who is trained to help.

Nobody knows how he or she will respond in an emergency until it happens. Role-playing a situation several times with babysitting friends or parents helps good ideas stick and can make the difference between panic and handling a situation calmly.

KNOW THE LAYOUT

Have the parents walk you through the house. Ask where the smoke alarms are located and if they have any established fire escape routes or instructions. Is there a fire extinguisher? If you smell smoke or the smoke alarm goes off, take the children and get out of the house as quickly as possible. Run to a neighbor's house to call the fire department. *Never* stop to call from the house if there is visible smoke or flames. Remember, the most important thing to do is get everyone out of the house *quickly*.

Keep your eyes open for light switches. Accidents are more likely to happen when you can't see what's ahead. Are there timers in the house that automatically turn lights off or on? There's nothing more startling than being in a new place and having a light or radio go on unexpectedly.

Is there a burglar alarm system? If you need to use it or turn it off, how does it work?

Where is the telephone? Is the emergency information posted? Are there paper and pencil near the phone for messages? Does this household have a telephone-answering machine? If so, request that it be turned on while you're sitting. This way, when the phone rings, you can screen the call. Make sure you know how to do that.

If there isn't an answering machine, remember phone safety. Let the caller know that Mr. and Mrs. Customer are not *available,* but you will be glad to take a message and have them return the call when they're free. If it's an urgent call, you will know and can relay the message. But *don't* tell the caller you are a babysitter, or what time you expect the children's parents. Don't give out *any* information about the household. Don't even repeat the phone number where you are. If someone thinks he's dialed the wrong number, ask him what number he dialed.

Are there any rules about answering the door? For instance, is there a relative who may drop by unexpectedly? Who can be allowed entrance? Ask for a description of anyone who can come in. If someone other than the parent is going to relieve you, how will it be handled?

If people aren't expected, is it okay to pretend not to be home? Is there a peephole in the door? Unless you have specific instructions, do not open the door to anyone you don't know.

Keep doors locked at all times. Unlocked doors, day or night, are an invitation to unwanted visitors. Make sure you know how the door locks work and test them. Cynthia was locked out of the house with her two charges because she didn't know that she had to pull the door toward her for the key to turn the lock.

Outside lights are a wonderful deterrent to intruders at night. But lights inside a house with the drapes open is a different story. Even a small lamp illuminates a room like stage lights in a theater. If it's dark enough to turn on a light, be sure to close the drapes.

BABY SAFETY

The good thing about new babies is if you use common sense it's relatively easy to keep them safe. But even small infants can throw themselves out of your arms, so always hold them with both hands.

Crawling babies are explorers and investigators. Since they don't know the danger around them, they need supervision every minute they're awake. Scan the play area for electrical cords, wobbly furniture, and anything that can be pulled over on the child. Anthony was four months old when he grabbed a stool. It fell on him and broke his collar bone.

Babies put everything in their mouths, so remove any objects that are smaller than the child's fist.

Another safety tip you might find useful if the parents use cloth diapers and pins is to shove the diaper pins into a bar of soap above the baby's head. The pins are out of the baby's sight and will slip more easily into the new diaper.

If the phone rings while you are diapering a baby, let it ring. Do not leave the baby alone, even for a second.

Don't leave a baby on a diapering table even if he or she is belted in. A healthy baby can kick his or her way into unsafe positions. Don't leave a newborn unattended on a sofa or bed either. Some babies are born with the crawling instinct and never lose it. The only safe places to leave awake, unsupervised babies are in cribs or playpens.

If the baby likes a warm bottle, don't heat it in a microwave oven. Although the outside of the bottle may feel cool, the milk could be scalding. Instead, put the bottle in a saucepan of hot tap water and warm under a low heat for a few minutes. Or pour milk into a glass container and heat it slightly in the microwave; pour it back into the bottle. Also, don't reuse plastic bottle liners or save bottles from one feeding to the next. The milk may become contaminated.

Test the warmth of the milk by shaking a few drops onto your wrist. Don't try to test for heat or cold with your fingers. Your fingers have a thicker layer of skin and are less sensitive.

GOOD GIRL, AMANDA, YOU'RE DRINKING YOUR WHOLE BOTTLE...
VIDEO TAPE
ANNE CANEVARI GREEN

A very young baby can choke on a propped bottle. Even if the baby is old enough to hold his or her own bottle, don't leave a little one alone to drink it. The best policy is to cradle the child in your arms or on your lap. Babies love cuddling.

TODDLERS

Toddlers are probably the most difficult children to keep safe. They don't mean to be—they are merely curious about the world around them and want to investigate everything. They are also copycats, so keep that in mind at all times. If they see you eating, they want to eat. If you take an aspirin, they want one also. If you comb your hair, they follow suit.

Toddlers are ingenious for figuring out how to get to the highest place in the house or hiding in the smallest. The best advice? Don't leave toddlers alone for an instant. If you're in the kitchen making lunch, strap a toddler in his or her highchair. Give him or her a spoon and plastic cup for entertainment or some other toy.

Although a highchair can keep a child contained, it is not meant for restraint. If you need to leave the kitchen, take the child with you.

Don't underestimate toddlers just because they can't talk. Instead, watch their actions and the twinkle in their eye. Get down on the floor and play with them.

Children of this age still put things in their mouths. This is another reason for not turning your back on the child. If a child is choking, turn the child upside down and give a good swat right between the shoulder blades.

Most parents childproof kitchens and bathrooms, but if the medicine cabinet is not childproof, close the bathroom door. Make sure the child does not go near electric outlets. Many parents plug up these outlets, but keep the child away anyway. And, if there are stairs in the home, keep the child away from them unless you help the child go up and down. Most toddlers *love* stairs!

PRESCHOOL AND
SCHOOL AGE

Safety should be your primary concern when you babysit. Parents are counting on you to spot potential danger so it can be averted. Although you don't have to be in the same room with this age child every second, you must be aware of what he or she is doing and continue to check up periodically. The younger the child, the more you can use the noise level as a guide. When it's silent, investigate.

When children are allowed outside, find out what the rules of the house are. If the parents don't mention safety rules, don't be afraid to establish your own. For the younger child, it may be as simple as "stay in your own yard." Preschool children do best with company because they have an adventuresome spirit. If an older sister or brother agrees to watch this tyke, limit the time so the older sibling doesn't feel taken advantage of.

If your charges are outside, the best place for you to be is there with them. Don't count on them remembering safety rules like don't play in the street, don't chase a ball out of the yard, or don't go to someone's house without permission. It's easy to forget these things when you're having fun.

When youngsters ride tricycles or big wheels on sidewalks, you become the traffic controller, especially at driveways. Try to find a safe place for

OH, MRS. WILSON, THEY'RE SUCH ANGELS, YOU WOULDN'T EVEN KNOW THEY WERE HERE!
ANNE CANEVARI GREEN

children to ride wheeled toys: a schoolyard or park, so that if they're out of control, they won't end up in the street.

Some youngsters are very self-reliant. If parents allow a child like this to do something you're uncomfortable with, say so to the child. "I'm sorry. If you want to ride your bicycle without a helmet, you must wait until your parents get home."

The best way to keep children safe is to be aware of what is going on all the time. That means, if you are watching television or playing video games, the children should be watching or playing right along with you. If the children aren't involved, then you shouldn't get involved.

It's best to avoid anything that distracts your attention from the child. If you're the kind of reader who gets lost in a book, leave your book at home. And the only conversation you should get lost in is with one of your charges. This means *no* personal calls on the job and *no* boyfriend or girlfriend or other visitors in the house. Always remember that babysitting is a big responsibility. It takes all of your attention.

YOU'RE IMPORTANT, TOO

Your safety is just as important as the children's safety. Don't forget to take care of yourself and speak up when you need to.

If a customer is abusive to you in any way—verbally, physically, or sexually—do not tolerate this behavior. Even if you think you might have misunderstood what happened, talk it over with your parents or another adult whom you trust. Don't let the fear of losing your job, or independence, get you fenced into a bad situation.

If you are babysitting at night, make sure customers know that you need to be picked up and brought back home. When you are going home, let the driver know that you want him or her to wait until you have safely entered your house before he or she drives away. If you need another way home, plan an alternative with your parents.

Michaela and her parents have a code sentence that she uses if she feels she needs their help. "If the children's parents come home drunk or their car doesn't have seat belts, I tell them Mom called and said she had an errand in the neighborhood, so she'd pick me up and save them a trip. If they don't believe me, they can even talk to Mom when I call her. Most of the time, they're glad to get out of driving me home."

Even if you think it's a silly reason for wanting your parents to come get you, remember they want you to be safe.

CHAPTER

ten

A BABYSITTING KIT

A babysitting kit is a reflection of the kind of person you are. Have fun with it. Tuck things into it that you still enjoy. Let the child in you show. And don't be afraid to tell little children these are *your* toys, but you will share them until you go home. This is also your chance to reinforce the idea of sharing by letting the children know how much fun you are having while you share.

Ultimately, the best part of a babysitting kit is not things. It's you and your imagination. The following are some suggestions to activate that imagination.

INFANT DISTRACTION

Babies are learning from the moment they are born. Tuck things into your kit that encourage a baby to use his or her senses. Sound, sight, and touch are the easiest ones to appeal to at this young age.

For the sense of hearing, take along the nursery rhyme and song book that was your favorite

as a child. If you didn't have one, now's the time to find one. Look in the children's section of the library. Check secondhand bookstores.

A baby will also enjoy the sound of a music box.

For the sense of sight, if you have the patience, you can cut out bright-colored pieces of paper and make a mobile with string and a clotheshanger. Place the finished product out of the baby's reach. This not only encourages a child to use his or her muscles but it also keeps infant hands from reaching something that doesn't belong in the mouth.

For the sense of touch, gather large pieces of scrap material—velvet, terry cloth, fur, satin—anything that has an interesting texture. If you have time, you might want to make soft little pillows of each material in different shapes.

PRESCHOOL CHILD

Your imagination is your best friend. The secret to any project is, the more you have fun with it, the more the child will enjoy it. Fun is contagious.

Try a game of animal make-believe. Show the child an example. As an elephant, you might rest your nose on your shoulder and swing your arm like a trunk. Would you believe that doing a silly thing like this would teach children anything? It does.

To stretch the imagination, make up a story. Get your whole body into it. Do you remember when you were little? What was your favorite story? Use it as a guide and personalize it by using the child's name. Encourage the child to add to the story. Stories don't have to make a lot of sense. In fact, if the child says, "That's not true," congratulate her on how smart she is.

Books are always a good standby. Young children love stories that have colorful characters, bright pictures, and repetition of words or ideas. Do you have a secret desire to be an actor or an actress? Now's your chance.

Books are also a source of creative ideas for crafts for different age groups. There are crafts books at the library on paperfolding and papercrafts. Children will be happy learning how to fold or do simple things, so don't start out with anything too complicated. For instance, make a colorful paper hat with the magazine section of the newspaper. Or use folded colored paper and blunt scissors to create snowflakes and other interesting shapes. For a different effect, try tearing instead of cutting.

Crayons and coloring books are always a hit, especially if you color right along with the children.

Clay or play dough teaches children something about texture and shaping. They love to play with it and squish it between their fingers.

Paste or glue is another item that comes in handy. Bring along some old magazines and cut out objects that the youngster likes. Then make a collage. Or find a large picture in the magazine section of the newspaper to paste on cardboard and cut into a simple puzzle.

A collage can also be made with several food items such as colorful dry beans, pasta shapes like shells (large and small), macaroni, and brown and white rice. Be careful if there are infants or small toddlers around when you use these materials. They can easily find their way into a little one's mouth. The messier the project, the better children like it. Be sure to bring along an old shirt to cover their clothes. Protect the surface you are working on with plastic garbage bags and/or newspapers and clean up afterward.

No matter what you do with children, you are the teacher. Just by the fact that you are older, little ones look up to you. If they truly admire you, they will usually copy things you do.

A parent put it this way: "The most challenging thing about being a parent is being a good example." Substitute the word *babysitter* for the word *parent* and it still applies.

THE SCHOOL-AGED CHILD

The older the child, the less important a physical babysitting kit is. Often, by the age of six, children already have favorite things to do. Ask them to show and tell you about their favorite activity. Then listen!

Tony has a business-card collection. Business cards may sound very dull to you, but Tony doesn't feel that way. There's excitement in his voice when he shows off his collection. He speaks of interesting people and unusual professions from several countries of the world.

Dogs are a favorite for Laura. She's taken her present dog through obedience training and dreams of showing him even though he's a mutt. Some day she intends to raise German shepherds.

John is interested in birds. Most of his knowledge came from working at a neighborhood game farm. He also has a private library on domestic and exotic feathered friends.

Children don't always share their interests because they think others will be critical or judgmental. There is nothing more depressing than having someone put down a project you find exciting. So, if you're less than enthusiastic about dolls or electronics, listen anyway. Every child is a learning experience.

For children who don't have any special interest, try a board game like Monopoly® or checkers. Or create your own game. Make cardboard cards and decorate them, making two of everything. Turn them face down, mix, then try to match.

Do you want to tickle their funnybone? Or let them tickle yours? Share the popular jokes of the day. Riddles and charades appeal to the child with imagination.

Don't be surprised if, at the beginning, you are the children's main interest. It's hard for them to believe that you were ever their age or that they will ever be your age. If you remember how you felt at their age, you will have an advantage, because you'll be more sensitive to their needs.

Taking an interest in what children like and who they are lets them know they are important to you. You are not so adult that you don't already know this. Having a friend who listens builds self-worth.

OUTSIDE ENTERTAINMENT

Who doesn't like soap bubbles? Their rainbow colors and the way they travel in the breeze are a fascination. They are best blown outside, but some parents will allow soap bubbles in the bathroom or kitchen.

Become an expert with a yo-yo, and you'll have children begging you to show them how.

Buy a paddleball or two. The ball is attached to the paddle with a length of rubber and it takes some skill, but not a lot, to hit the ball. This is a game that is fun, win or lose. In fact, the less skill you have, the better the youngsters like it. They catch on fast and contests can last for hours.

Jump rope to rhymes or jingles. Bring a couple of jump ropes in case youngsters don't have their own, and trade jingles.

Nature can also provide outside entertainment. Spread a blanket outside, lie back, and find animals in the clouds. Or make a picnic lunch, then fly a kite.

There's no end to the activities you can engage in by just using some imagination and creativity.

CHAPTER

SMART SITTERS

Most babysitters start out sitting for money. But smart sitters continue to sit because sitting is a giving tree. What the tree gives depends on the receiver.

It may be as simple as acceptance. LeVelle says that with little children, "You are free to be a silly person. They like you just the way you are."

In comparison, you have to gain an older youngster's trust. "It's neat when they accept you like a sister or a friend, confide in you, and ask for advice."

Savvy sitters say the tree offers self-esteem. "When people trust someone so dear to their hearts with you, it says you are a good person."

The tree gives greater self-confidence. One summer day Joe took his three charges out into the backyard and sat on a blanket with the baby. A squirrel unexpectedly appeared on the fence. Joe and the children watched it as it chattered and flitted its tail, then raced down the fence and stopped. Suddenly, the animal dashed at the baby. From that moment, Joe said, every action was in

freeze frame. He reached out, grabbed the squirrel by the tail, hurled the animal over the fence, and rushed the children inside.

The baby wasn't hurt, but Joe warned the parents and they spread the news around the neighborhood. Several days later, the squirrel was captured as it tried to attack another child.

Joe admits that he doesn't know how he did what he did, but he has more faith in himself and his ability to handle the unexpected now. (However, it is not recommended that you approach and pick up a squirrel.)

The giving tree, some sitters say, presents opportunities to become a child again, capturing polliwogs and stalking dragons. Children make them laugh, and help them take themselves less seriously.

Other sitters say they keep sitting because of the independence that the tree provides. They like being their own boss, learning skills in relationships, and forming friendships.

Though smart sitters know the tree doesn't offer the same for all, they do agree that the sitting giving tree keeps on giving and giving and giving.

APPENDIX

BABYSITTING CLASSES:
WHOM TO CALL
FOR INFORMATION

- Boys and girls clubs

- City park and recreation centers

- Schools

- Children's hospital or community hospital

- *Campfire Girls and Boys*—Beginning babysitting classes and a *Special Sitters* class. In *Special Sitters*, teens learn to care for developmentally delayed and disabled children.

- *Red Cross*—Most chapters don't have a babysitting course for youngsters, but they do maintain a list of Red Cross accredited classes offered in the community.

- Safe Sitter, a not-for-profit group, offers seminars for boys and girls eleven to thirteen on the basics, plus rescue techniques and how to handle choking. Call 1-800-255-4089 for more information.

FIRST AID CLASSES

- *Red Cross—Standard First Aid* course which includes cardio-pulmonary resuscitation (CPR). Call and ask for a schedule. Classes fill rapidly. There is a class fee, but scholarships are available for those who qualify.

CARDIO-PULMONARY
RESUSCITATION (CPR)

- *Fire Department*—Call for information and qualifying criteria.

FOR FURTHER READING

Barkin, Carol, and Elizabeth James. *The Complete Babysitter's Handbook.* New York: Wanderer Books, 1980.

Benton, Barbara. *The Babysitter's Handbook.* New York: Morrow, 1981.

Faucher, Elizabeth. *Adventures in Babysitting.* New York: Scholastic Inc., 1987.

Fletcher, Sarah. *Christian Babysitter's Handbook.* St. Louis, Missouri: Concordia, 1985.

Gilbert, Sara. *By Yourself.* New York: Lothrop, 1983.

Lansky, Vicki. *Dear Babysitter.* New York: Bantam, 1987.

Marsoli, Lisa. *Things to Know Before You Babysit.* Morristown, New Jersey: Silver Burdett & Ginn, 1985.

Saunders, Rubie. *Baby Sitting for Fun & Profit.* New York: Archway, 1984.

Stine, Jane, and Jovial B. Stine. *Everything You Need to Survive: Brothers & Sisters.* New York: Random House, 1983.

INDEX

ABOUT THE AUTHOR

Frances S. Dayee, the mother of thirteen children and the grandmother of six, is a native of the Pacific Northwest. She lives in Washington State with her husband and five of their youngsters.

Her chief interests are children, animals, camping, nature, and reading.

Dayee has been a department store sales clerk, a phone company mail clerk, a free-lance writer, and a writing teacher for youngsters and adults. The interaction between her and young students, combined with experiences of children in her immediate family, verifies her belief that it pays to listen to the younger generation.

Dayee has been involved in babysitting or with babysitters for forty years, first as a teen sitter, then as a nanny, later as a parent hiring sitters, and, finally, a parent supplying sitters. This book is the result of interviewing the experts, teen sitters, their charges, and parents of both.

Dayee's writing reflects her love of and respect for children. She has written for and about children since 1978. Her column, *Love and Popcorn*, focuses on the positive aspects of preschool children. She was the editor of *Kid's Korner*, a children's column in a newspaper, and a contributing editor and stringer for several publications.

Her previous books, *Private Zone* and *Smart Plays*, supply youngsters with child abuse defenses.